# KNITS
## from the North Sea

lace in the shetland tradition

Carol Rasmussen Noble
and Margaret Leask Peterson

*Martingale*®
& COMPANY

# DEDICATIONS

To Mary Jean Peterson ~ Margaret

To my father ~ Carol

# ACKNOWLEDGMENTS

Thank you above all to Mary Green at Martingale & Company for her openness to the idea for this book, and to our editor, Karen Soltys, who helped bring it about. A special thank you, also, to Carol's husband for typing the manuscript. Margaret feels a great debt to Mary Jean Peterson, who was her lace mentor, and to her grandson, Logan Spence, for his support. Carol wishes to thank Margaret Dalrymple and Claudia Judson Chesney for their support throughout the entire project.

Knits from the North Sea: Lace in the Shetland Tradition
© 2009 by Carol Rasmussen Noble and Margaret Leask Peterson

Martingale & Company
20205 144th Ave. NE
Woodinville, WA 98072-8478 USA
www.martingale-pub.com

Printed in China

14 13 12 11 10 09   8 7 6 5 4 3 2 1

**Library of Congress Cataloging-in-Publication Data**
Library of Congress Control Nmber: 2009013172

ISBN: 978-1-56477-832-1

## Credits

President & CEO: Tom Wierzbicki

Editor in Chief: Mary V. Green

Managing Editor: Tina Cook

Developmental & Technical Editor: Karen Costello Soltys

Copy Editor: Sheila Chapman Ryan

Design Director: Stan Green

Production Manager: Regina Girard

Illustrators: Robin Strobel & Laurel Strand

Cover & Text Designer: Shelly Garrison

Photographer: Brent Kane

## Mission Statement

Dedicated to providing quality products and service to inspire creativity.

**Scrapbook Papers Used in Book Design**
Autumn Leaves, a Division of Creativity Inc.: C'est Pink #7001 by Rhonna Farrer
Fancy Pants Designs, Inc.: Appealing #863 by Michelle Coleman; Sweet Nothings #851 by Nancie Rowe-Janitz
My Mind's Eye: Bohemia Bluebird Birthday

# contents

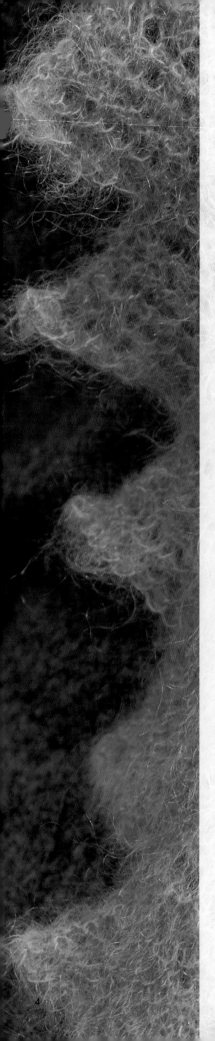

# introduction

Margaret asked me to write an introduction for both of us, which is easy because we speak with one voice: lace is our passion. I first met Margaret in 1996 in Shetland, and we instantly formed a bond. Margaret is a world-renowned lace knitter. By my third visit to Shetland in 2001, we were close friends. On that visit I asked her to take me on as a lace student. Thinking back, she says she looked into my eyes and saw that I could be a great lace knitter. And so she said yes. But she did not teach me to knit *her* lace—she taught me to knit *my* lace.

Margaret and I share the creative gift of visualization. We each see our designs fully finished in our minds, and then must work backward to plan out the knitting. From this point we differ. My reverse engineering starts with the construction of graphs, but Margaret has the ability to do it all in her head. Amazingly, prior to this book she had never worked with a graph or chart.

Margaret's lace is pure Unst: Shetland lace that is highly sophisticated in layout but often simple technically. (Unst is the northernmost populated island of the British Islands.) My lace, with its Shetland and Orenburg, Russia, roots, is simple in layout but in many instances a bit more complex technically. But that's the beauty of lace knitting—it accommodates everyone's style. Lace is a pathway for all knitters no matter their skill levels or experience. We have tried very hard to reflect this in our book—there is something for everyone here. And we hope that you will enjoy making these projects as much as we did. After all, knitting lace is prayer and discipline combined. It is pure joy.

~ Carol Rasmussen Noble

# TIPS and TECHNIQUES for lace knitting

In its simplest form, lace knitting incorporates knit and purl stitches along with yarn overs to form openwork. Lace knitting also uses two stitches worked together to maintain an even stitch count. That said, lace knitting also requires a bit of finesse, the right tools, and special techniques. The information presented here will help beginning lace knitters get off to a good start and may even provide some insight to the more experienced lace knitter.

## LACE YARNS

When choosing a lace yarn, I look for a weight-yardage ratio of at least 400 yards to 50 grams that is meant to be knit on size 1 or 2 needles. Knitting this lightweight type of yarn on larger needles would produce holes that are too big and droopy.

If you prefer knitting on needles that are larger than size 2, you can make a very nice wrap using fingering-weight yarn on size 3 or 4 needles. But personally, I feel that's the upper size limit, and the projects in this book reflect this guideline.

I like to use animal fibers—merino wool, baby mohair, cashmere, qiviut, or alpaca—preferably combined with silk. Silk gives the yarn a glow because it takes dyes so well, it reduces stretch, and in general it makes the yarn easier to work with. Cotton yarns, which work well for some projects, tend to be limp and don't drape well in a lace garment. Other plant-based fibers, such as soysilk, tencel, or rayon, can pill a lot and they have no give, so I don't use them for lacework.

When it comes to color, lace is lovely in all sorts of shades from pure white and pastels to mid-tones, jewel tones, and very dark colors. The yarns used in this book reflect a wide variety of colors, but please feel free to select whatever color you like best. You might even find a slightly mottled or variegated yarn that works well, but yarns with great contrast are not the best option since the color changes can obscure the intricate lace patterns.

In each project, Margaret and I list the type of yarn used along with a yarn-weight icon, which indicates the weight of the yarn used. You can use this information for substituting another yarn to ensure that your project will turn out to be the same size and gauge as the project shown. Below is a description of the yarn weights and icons.

| YARN WEIGHTS | | | | |
|---|---|---|---|---|
| Yarn-Weight Symbol and Category Name | **0** Lace | **1** Super Fine | **2** Fine | **3** Light |
| Types of Yarn in Category | Fingering, 10-count crochet thread | Sock, Fingering, Baby | Sport, Baby | DK, Light Worsted |
| Knit Gauge Range* in Stockinette Stitch to 4" | 33 to 40 sts | 27 to 32 sts | 23 to 26 sts | 21 to 24 sts |
| Recommended Needle in U.S. Size Range | 000 to 1 | 1 to 3 | 3 to 5 | 5 to 7 |
| Recommended Needle in Metric Size Range | 1.5 to 2.25 mm | 2.25 to 3.25 mm | 3.25 to 3.75 mm | 3.75 to 4.5 mm |

*These are guidelines only. The above reflect the most commonly used gauges and needle sizes for specific yarn categories.

# NEEDLES

In my long search for needles that neither bend nor break, I have finally settled on metal ones. I recommend single-point metal needles that are 10" long or shorter for all lace knitting. There are a number of good brands available, and you don't have to buy the most expensive ones to get the best needle. You can also use two double-pointed needles with point protectors on the ends. Personally, I use Inox 10" single-point needles. I highly recommend that you don't knit lace on circular needles because the points and cords are different diameters and made of different materials, so they can't hold stitches at an even tension. This unevenness will show in your finished work. It's important to knit lace with medium, even tension, and be consistent. Uneven tension shows up most obviously as different hole sizes.

| KNITTING NEEDLE SIZES | |
|---|---|
| DIAMETER IN MILLIMETERS | U.S. SIZE |
| 2 mm | 0 |
| 2.25 mm | 1 |
| 2.75 mm | 2 |
| 3.25 mm | 3 |
| 3.5 mm | 4 |
| 3.75 mm | 5 |
| 4 mm | 6 |
| 4.5 mm | 7 |
| 5 mm | 8 |

## READING A CHART

On knitting stitch charts, right-side rows are read from right to left and wrong-side rows are read from left to right. In many cases, charts may show stitches at each edge to be worked only once on each row, with a block of stitches that are to be repeated a specified number of times in between. Each pattern will detail for you how to read its particular charts and specify how many repeats to work.

# MARKERS AND COUNTING

Place stitch markers between each repeat section on your needle. Use small, non-bulky, non-dangling markers so that they don't become tangled in the holes in the lace. Markers are an aid to counting. It is essential that you count as you knit to avoid mistakes in the lace pattern. In addition to keeping track of the number of stitches in a horizontal repeat, you'll need to keep track of both the rows within a repeat and the number of vertical repeats. Try using two row counters of different sizes or colors on a string around your neck. This worked for me when I was starting lace knitting. Above all, when making lace you must not lose your place. When you put your work down for any length of time, it's a good idea to note in writing on your pattern where you left off.

## UNEVEN STITCH COUNTS

Sometimes in a charted pattern, a yarn over appears at one side of the marker and a decrease at the other (representing the end of one horizontal repeat and the beginning of the next). In this case, you'll need to slip one or more stitches from one side of the marker to the other to knit your repeats correctly. This is not a mistake in the pattern or in your work; it's simply a matter of where the decrease needs to occur in the pattern. The chart will show you what the finished repeats should look like.

## SKILL LEVELS

I've assigned a skill level to each of the projects in this book. While I've used the same general ratings as adopted by the Craft Yarn Council, I've modified the description just a bit. According to those guidelines, any lace knitting immediately becomes classified as "Intermediate" or "Experienced." However, I feel that some of the projects in this book are a bit less complicated than others and have therefore assigned them an "Easy" ranking. This does not mean that they are suitable for an absolute beginner knitter, but they are easier than the rest of the projects in the book, and if this is your first outing with a lace project, you might want to start with one of those.

Below is how I've defined the skill levels as they apply to the projects in this book.

◼◼◻◻ **Easy:** Projects for first-time lace knitters using basic stitches: knit, purl, yarn over, and simple decreases such as knitting two stitches together and slip, slip, knit.

◼◼◼◻ **Intermediate:** Projects using a variety of stitches, such as basic lace, simple intarsia, and grafting.

◼◼◼▶ **Experienced:** Projects using more complex techniques and stitches, such as short rows, more intricate lace patterns, and numerous color changes.

## ADDING ON NEW YARN

When adding on a new ball of yarn, tie it on with an overhand knot.

Believe me, the knot will not show in your finished piece, and your lace will be stronger and more durable. *Do not* tie on a new ball right at the edge as you would when knitting a sweater or other garment with seams. Start a new ball an inch or so in from the edge because knots right at an edge are harder to hide. They also interfere with knitting on a border.

## CORRECTING ERRORS

The best way to catch errors early is to carefully count each repeat after you've knit it. If your count is off, you instantly know that you've made a mistake. Comparing your stitches to those shown on the chart will show you where you went wrong. Then you can easily correct the error.

If you must rip out, do not remove the needles to unravel the yarn; this will be disastrous. Instead, take out the stitches one at a time, keeping all stitches on the needles. It will seem tedious, but it's the only way to manage the task. Take special care that you do not lose your yarn overs as you unknit.

## RUSSIAN GRAFTING

Russian grafting is a method of joining two pieces of lace seamlessly by grafting live stitches on one needle to the same number of live stitches on a second needle. For example, when knitting a lace scarf that has a directional pattern, you want the pattern to head in the same direction on both ends of the scarf for a symmetrical look. You'll knit two identical pieces and join them at the middle of the scarf using Russian grafting so that you don't have a seam showing.

1. Start with the wrong side of each piece facing you and with the needles pointing toward one another. (The working ends of the yarn should be at the point end of each needle, so you'll have to work one extra row on one of the pieces to get to this position.) Insert the left needle into the first two stitches on the right needle. Pull the second stitch on the right needle through the first stitch.

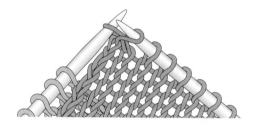

2. Slip this pulled-through stitch onto the left needle; then drop the original first stitch on the right needle.

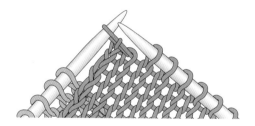

3. Next, insert the point of the right needle through the first two stitches on the left needle. Pull the second stitch through the first stitch and slip it to the right needle. Then drop this first stitch.

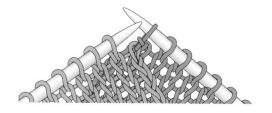

4. Continue in this manner, working back and forth pulling the second stitch through the first stitch on the right needle and then on the left. The join will look like a herringbone weave.

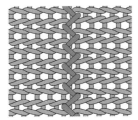

5. When you have just one stitch left on the needle, thread a piece of your lace yarn through it and tie a square knot. Weave in the ends.

## INTARSIA

Intarsia is a technique in which you use more than one color discontinuously in a row. In other words, you use one color, drop it, use another color, and then go back to the first color or change to a third color, and so on. Because the spacing between color changes is too large to strand the color not in use along the back of the work, for intarsia you need to work from separate balls of yarn or bobbins at each place where the new color is added. To avoid tangles, it is best to use bobbins for each color area. If you have only a few large color areas, you can knit off balls or cones.

When changing colors, simply knit across the row using color A, twist colors A and B, drop A, and continue knitting with color B. Be sure to always twist the yarns when you change colors to avoid creating a hole.

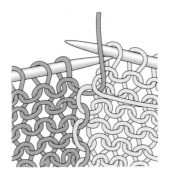

## PROVISIONAL CAST ON

A provisional cast on worked with waste yarn is used as a base edge for your piece when you need live stitches along the starting edge so that you can come back later and knit on a border. By doing so, you'll have a seamless edge where the border joins the body of the work, rather than a ridge that will form if you go back and pick up stitches along a cast-on edge.

For waste yarn, I always use fine white crochet cotton because it is smooth and easy to see when you go to cut it away. However, if your project yarn is white, a pastel crochet cotton would make it easier for you to see the cast-on stitches when it's time to remove them.

To start, simply cast on as usual using the waste yarn. When all the stitches have been cast on, cut the waste yarn and tie on your lace yarn. You're now ready to begin row 1 of your lace pattern.

Leave the provisional cast on in place until you are ready to knit the border to the cast-on edge. To release the stitches, you need sharp scissors with a long, sharp point and a fine crochet hook. Turn the piece to the wrong side. Working one stitch at a time, snip each waste yarn stitch with scissors to pull it out. Then pick up the body stitch you just released onto your needle. I recommend making as few snips as possible and using your crochet hook to work out the waste yarn. This lessens the possibility of accidentally cutting the lace yarn. If you should accidentally cut the lace yarn, don't disturb the yarn ends. When you come to this spot while working your border, pick up the stitch you need from the row below.

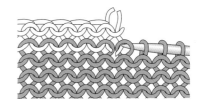

# KNITTING ON A BORDER

Some of the projects in this book have borders knit onto the main work. When you complete the knitting for your project, don't bind off the stitches. You start with a left-hand needle full of live stitches.

1. Using the same yarn that's already attached, hold the needle with the live stitches in your left hand. On the tip of this needle, cast on the number of stitches specified for your border pattern. Working on the cast-on stitches, knit row 1 of your border pattern up to, but not including, the last cast-on stitch.

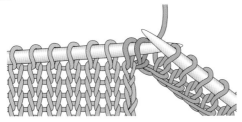

2. Knit this last cast-on stitch together with the first stitch of the body.

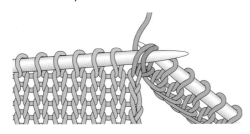

3. Turn your work. Slip the knit-together stitch purlwise onto the right needle. Finish row 2 of your border pattern.

4. Turn your work and repeat the process, working rows 3 and 4 of your border pattern, and so on. On every right-side (odd-numbered) row, you'll knit the last stitch of the border together with the next live stitch of the garment.

## Working a Border Corner

Prior to knitting on the border, your piece of knitted lace will have live stitches at the top edge, a provisional cast on at the bottom edge, and two side edges. Start the border at the top edge where you have live stitches and work around.

A border needs to curve evenly around the corners of the work. If the border is worked too tightly around the corner, the border will pucker rather than lie flat. The trick to achieving nicely rounded corners is to use short rows. You will work two full rows and two short rows into one stitch on the lace piece. (Keep in mind that normally one stitch accommodates two full border rows.) This is the basic corner unit. If your pattern calls for three corner stitches, you'll need to work this corner unit into each of three edge stitches. Work the short-row corners as follows.

1. Work rows 1 and 2 of your border pattern normally. On row 3 of the border, knit to within one stitch of the end of the row.

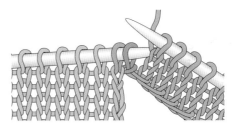

2. Turn your work. Slip the first stitch purlwise onto the right needle.

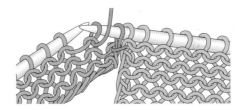

3. Complete row 4 of the border pattern. Now begin the process all over again with the second body stitch and row 5 of your border.

This short-row process is repeated a specified number of times at the beginning and end of each edge for border corners, as described in the project directions.

## Picking Up Stitches along a Side Edge

After the first corner has been worked, you'll need to pick up stitches along the adjacent side edge. To pick up stitches along a side edge, use the needle that has only border stitches on it to pick up every loop along the adjacent side edge. (The loops result from slipping the first stitch of every row purlwise, and accommodate two body rows each; you are slipping the loop onto the needle, not pulling a tail of yarn through the loop.) When all the loops along the edge are on your needle, use your other needle and, working back toward the start of the edge, twist every loop by inserting the point of the right needle into the back of the loop and slipping it from the left to the right needle.

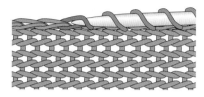

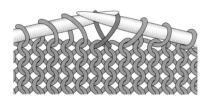

Your stitches are now in the correct position for knitting into as you work the border. Treating each twisted loop as a body stitch, knit on the border as described in "Knitting On a Border" (page 9).

## Decreasing and Increasing along an Edge

Sometimes when knitting on a border, it's necessary to increase or decrease a stitch along the side of the work to accommodate the border-pattern row repeat. For example, when you pick up each loop on the side of your shawl, you may have 485 stitches. But if your border repeat is 10 rows, you need to have a multiple of 10 for your stitch count. In this case, you'd need to either increase or decrease 5 stitches to accommodate an even number of border motifs. Each pattern in this book will specify how many stitches, if any, you'll need to increase or decrease.

To decrease one stitch along an edge when knitting on a border, knit the last stitch of your border row together with two body stitches. To increase one stitch along an edge, use short rows like you were working a corner (see page 9).

## BLOCKING

Before blocking, weave in all ends for 1" using a crochet hook. I have tried a number of blocking methods and have had the greatest success with blocking wires. These can be purchased as a set. When using wires, it is easier to start with a dry piece of knitting.

For a piece with knitted-on borders, run the wires through the tips of the border points. If one wire is not long enough for the entire edge, use two and overlap them by at least 12". If your piece does not have a knitted-on border, thread the wires through every loop on the side edges and every stitch on the ends.

Lay out your piece with wires on a flat surface such as a bed, carpet, or blocking board and anchor the wires with T-pins placed every 8" to 10" to block the project to the finished dimensions.

Using a sprayer full of water, wet the lace thoroughly. A small, inexpensive hand-pumped pressurized sprayer (similar to those used for applying herbicides) works very well and takes much less time and effort than using a hand-squeezed spray bottle. Allow the piece to completely dry and set for two days before removing the pins and wires.

## WASHING

To wash lace, I always soak it overnight in cold water with a generous amount of baby shampoo that is free of additives. Rinse well in cold water, handling the piece gently. Then roll up the lace in a towel and gently squeeze out excess moisture. Block as described above for dry lace, even though the piece is still wet.

As an alternative, you might want to try one of the newer products made specifically for washing handknits. I love the results I get using baby shampoo, but these specialty products don't require rinsing before gently squeezing out the excess water.

# SCARVES

Scarves are wonderfully versatile—you can wear them to highlight a multitude of outfits for both indoor and outdoor wear. They're also perfect for learning lace knitting because they're easier to handle and faster to finish than larger projects.

# carol's mountain stream SCARF

Picture a mountain stream rushing over rocks and reflecting a deep blue mountain sky. That majestic scenery is what I knit into this scarf. Although the design looks difficult to knit, it is actually deceptively easy and makes a dramatic scarf.

**Skill level:** ◨■□□

**Dimensions:** 7½" x 48" measured at widest point; 5" wide at inner points

**Gauge:** 7½ sts and 10 rows = 1"

## MATERIALS

2 skeins of Douceur et Soie from Knit One, Crochet Too (65% baby mohair, 35% silk; 25 g; 225 yds) in color 8633 Cornflower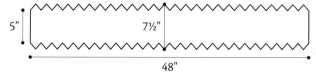

Size 1 (2.25 mm) needles

2 stitch markers

## PATTERN

CO 38 sts. K17, pm, K4, pm, K17 sts.

Knit 1 row (WS).

Working from chart (page 15), work rows 1–19.

Rep, working only rows 2–19 for all reps until you have worked 25 vertical patt reps.

Work 1 more vertical rep, working rows 2–18. Then work row 20.

Knit 1 row.

BO loosely.

## FINISHING

Weave in ends. Do not block. Dry clean only.

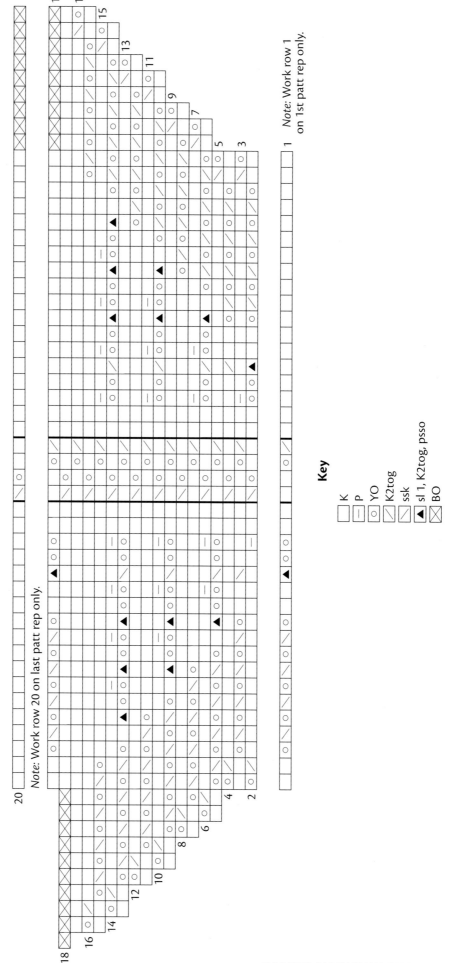

**Key**

| | |
|---|---|
| ☐ | K |
| ⏤ | P |
| ○ | YO |
| ╱ | K2tog |
| ╲ | ssk |
| ◀ | sl 1, K2tog, psso |
| ☒ | BO |

*Note:* Work row 1 on 1st patt rep only.

*Note:* Work row 20 on last patt rep only.

# carol's peaches and cream SCARF

For this design, I used the Russian pattern called peas. Although the yarn is fine, it is easy to work with and makes the scarf easy to knit. To me, this scarf is an allover peach delight.

**Skill level:** ◼◼◻◻

**Dimensions:** 9" x 48"

**Gauge:** 7 sts and 12 rows = 1"

## MATERIALS

3 skeins of Douceur et Soie from Knit One, Crochet Too (65% baby mohair, 35% silk; 25 g; 225 yds) in color 8320 Cantaloupe [1]

Size 1 (2.25 mm) needles

14 stitch markers

## PATTERN

CO 62 sts. Knit 4 rows.

On next row (RS), beg patt working from chart below. The first 2 rows are knit only. On row 3, est patt by working 5 beg sts, pm, work 13 reps of 4-st patt, pm bet each rep; work 5 end sts. Cont in patt until you've worked 72 vertical reps of the 8-row patt.

Knit 6 rows.

BO loosely.

## FINISHING

Weave in ends. Do not block. Dry clean only.

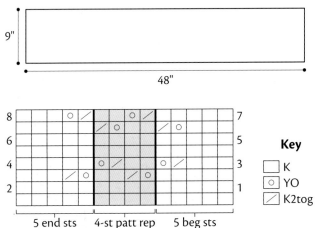

**Key**

| | |
|---|---|
| ☐ | K |
| ⊙ | YO |
| ╱ | K2tog |

5 end sts    4-st patt rep    5 beg sts

# margaret's cockleshell
# SCARF

Cockleshell is a traditional Shetland pattern used for scarves, usually knit as an allover pattern. In this coat scarf, Margaret combines the cockleshells with an attractive mesh to give a contrast in texture. The scarf is knit in halves that are grafted together so that each end of the scarf will be identical when worn. To make the scarf longer, simply knit more repeats on each half of the scarf.

**Skill level:** ◼◼◼◻

**Dimensions:** 14" x 46"

**Gauge:** 6 sts and 10 rows = 1" in cockleshell patt

## MATERIALS

2 balls of Matchmaker Merino 4-Ply from Jaeger (100% merino wool; 50 g; 200 yds) in color 701 Heather, or other fingering-weight merino yarn such as Rowan 4-Ply Soft (50 g; 191 yds) or Baby Ull from Dale of Norway (50 g; 180 yds) 🔳

2 pairs of size 3 (3.25 mm) needles

10 stitch markers

## SECTION 1

CO 78 sts.

Work set-up row as foll, refer to Chart B on page 21: K1; pm; work 5 reps of chart B; pm; K21 (row 1 of chart A); pm; work 7 reps of chart B; pm; K21 (row 1 of chart A); pm; work 5 reps of chart B; K1.

Cont in patt, always knitting 1 st on each edge, until you've worked 13 vertical reps of chart A.

Leave sts on spare needle.

## SECTION 2

Work as for section 1. Work row 1 of patt again.

Align the two sections so that needles point toward one another and with both wrong sides facing you. Use Russian grafting (page 7) to join sections.

## FINISHING

Weave in ends and block (page 10).

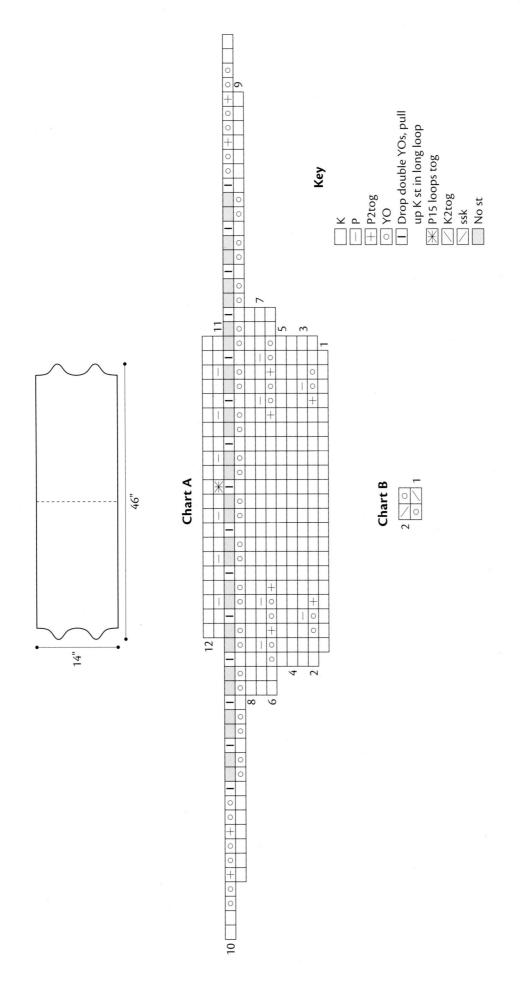

**Chart A**

**Chart B**

**Key**

| | K |
| | P |
| | P2tog |
| | YO |
| | Drop double YOs, pull up K st in long loop |
| | P15 loops tog |
| | K2tog |
| | ssk |
| | No st |

46"

14"

# carol's dawn mist SCARF

When I first saw this yarn, I pictured mauve mist sparkling in the dawn light. And so this design was born. Lovely to wear and easy to knit—this project has it all.

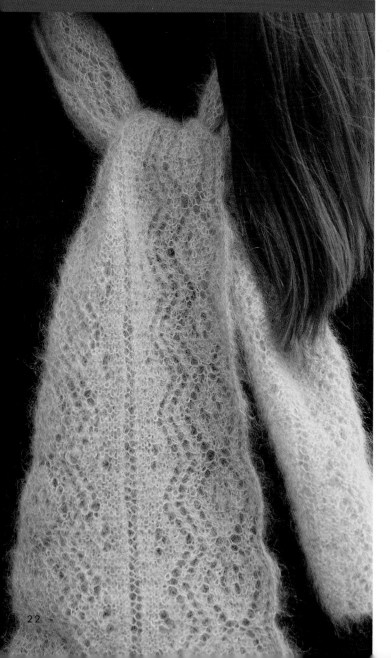

**Skill level:** ◼◼◼◻

**Dimensions:** 6½" x 48½"

**Gauge:** 6¾ sts and 11 rows = 1"

## MATERIALS

2 skeins of Douceur et Soie from Knit One, Crochet Too (65% baby mohair, 35% silk; 25 g; 225 yds) in color 8248 Velvet Rose **1**

Size 1 (2.25 mm) needles

3 stitch markers

## PATTERN

CO 44 sts.

**Set-up row (RS):** K18; pm; K8; pm; K18.

**Next row:** Knit.

Using chart on page 25, set up lace patt as foll:

Work row 1 of chart. This row is worked only once. For vertical patt repeats, work rows 2–21. Continue in this manner until you have worked 26 vertical reps. On last row of 26th vertical rep, omit row 21 and work row 22 as indicated on chart.

Knit 1 row.

BO loosely.

## FINISHING

Weave in ends. Do not block. Dry clean only.

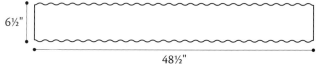

6½"

48½"

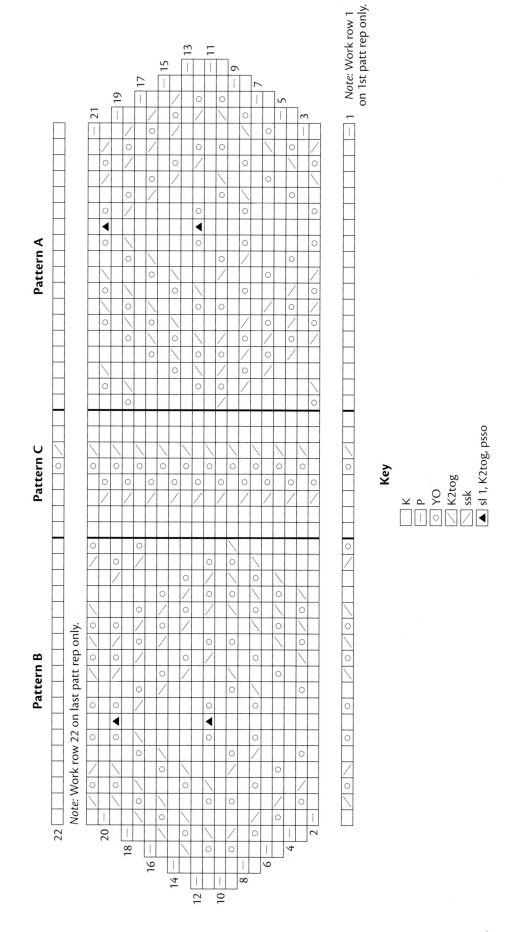

**Pattern A**

21
19
17
15
13
11
9
7
5
3

**Pattern C**

**Pattern B**

*Note:* Work row 22 on last patt rep only.

22
20
18
16
14
12
10
8
6
4
2

1

*Note:* Work row 1 on 1st patt rep only.

**Key**

| | K |
|---|---|
| — | P |
| ○ | YO |
| / | K2tog |
| \ | ssk |
| ◀ | sl 1, K2tog, psso |

# margaret's starry night SCARF

This coat scarf features star motifs at each end with rays of starlight in between. The scarf is knit in two pieces that are grafted together. If you'd like a longer scarf, you can easily lengthen it by making the ribbing section longer, although you would need one additional ball of yarn to do so.

**Skill level:** ◼◼◼◻

**Dimensions:** 13" x 30½"

**Gauge:** 6 sts and 10 rows = 1"

## MATERIALS

2 balls of Matchmaker Merino 4-Ply from Jaeger (100% merino wool; 50 g; 200 yds) in color 740 Baltic Blue, or other fingering-weight merino yarn such as Rowan 4-Ply Soft (50 g; 191 yds) or Baby Ull from Dale of Norway (50 g; 180 yds) ◼**3**◼

2 pairs of size 3 (3.25 mm) needles

14 stitch markers

Patt rep = 10 sts plus 16

## SECTION 1

The scarf is knit in 2 pieces that are grafted together. The first piece is worked in 3 different patts (edging, lace motif, and ribbing) foll charts A, B, and C (page 29). The second piece uses only edging and lace stitches.

### Bottom Edging (Chart A)

CO 85 sts.

**Set-up row:** Work 13 beg sts, pm, work 6 full reps of patt sts (pm bet each rep), work 12 end sts.

**Rows 2–8:** Work rem 7 rows of chart A to complete edging.

## Lace Motifs (Chart B)

Work 3 vertical reps of chart B.

## Vertical Ribbing (Chart C)

Work 58 vertical reps of chart C (or until rib section is desired length). Leave sts on spare needle.

## SECTION 2

CO 85 sts and work as for first scarf section through 3 vertical reps of chart B. Knit 1 row.

## FINISHING

Align scarf sections with needles pointing toward one another and wrong sides facing you. Join using Russian grafting (page 7).

Weave in ends and block (page 10).

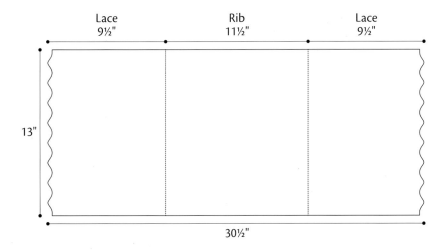

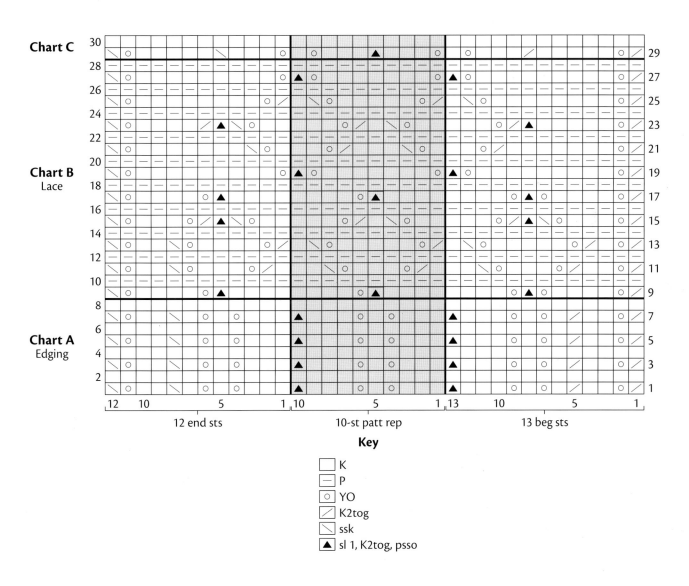

**Key**

| | |
|---|---|
| ☐ | K |
| — | P |
| ⊙ | YO |
| ╱ | K2tog |
| ╲ | ssk |
| ▲ | sl 1, K2tog, psso |

# carol's ruffles
# SCARF

The yarn used for this scarf is a lovely blend of baby mohair and silk; it makes a fluffy, luxurious lace. Although the yarn is very fine, it is easy to work with, and needs no blocking. This scarf makes a dramatic statement.

**Skill level:** ■■□□

**Dimensions:** 6¾" x 48"

**Gauge:** 7 sts and 10½ rows = 1"

## MATERIALS

2 skeins of Douceur et Soie from Knit One, Crochet Too (65% baby mohair, 35% silk; 25 g; 225 yds) in color 8359 Pimento **1**

Size 1 (2.25 mm) needles

2 stitch markers

## PATTERN

CO 46 sts.

**Set-up row (RS):** K20; pm; K6; pm; K20.

**Next row:** Knit.

Using chart on page 32, work row 1 of chart. This row is worked only once. For vertical patt reps, work rows 2–9. Continue in this manner until you have worked 62 vertical reps. On last row of 62nd vertical rep, omit row 9 and work "Last Row" as indicated on chart.

Knit 2 rows.

BO loosely.

## FINISHING

Weave in ends. Do not block. Dry clean only.

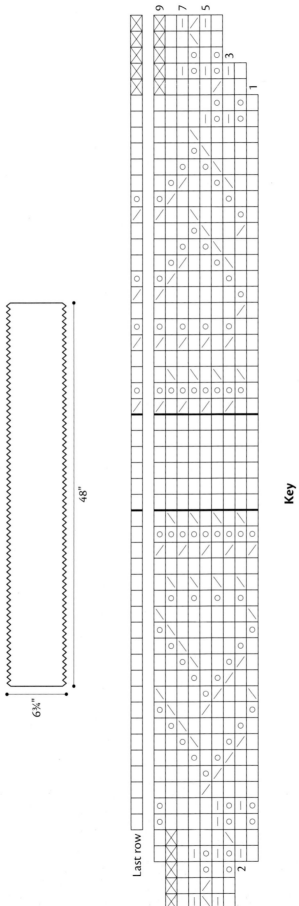

Last row

48"

6¾"

**Key**

K
P
YO
K2tog
ssk
BO

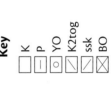

9 7 5 3 1

8 6 4 2

# carol's spiderweb SCARF

I adapted this design from a photograph of a piece of old Shetland lace that I found in a reference book. The intricate lace details contrast nicely with the garter-stitch bands. The border, which is knit on after the rectangle is complete, is also traditional Shetland.

**Skill level:** ■■■□

**Dimensions:** 16½" x 62"

**Gauge:** 7 sts and 14 rows = 1"

## MATERIALS

2 balls of Zephyr from JaggerSpun (50% merino wool, 50% tussah silk; 2 oz; 630 yds) in color Violet **2**

Size 2 (2.75 mm) needles

8 stitch markers

Waste yarn

## SCARF PATTERN

CO 97 sts using waste yarn for provisional CO (page 8).

Knit 30 rows.

On next row (RS), set up patt from chart A (page 36) as foll: work 20 beg st of chart; pm; work 5 reps of 14-st patt rep (pm bet each rep); work 7 end sts.

Work in patt for 26 rows, foll by 30 rows of garter st.

Alternating plain bands and lace bands, work total of 11 lace bands and end with 30 garter-st rows. *Do not bind off.*

## BORDER

Referring to "Knitting On a Border" (page 9), CO 9 sts on end of needle with live scarf sts and begin working border patt foll chart B (page 36).

Work corners over 3 sts at beg and end of each edge, referring to "Working a Border Corner" (page 8).

On top and bottom edges, you will have 97 sts; dec 1 st on each of these edges as you work border so that you have 96 sts per edge. (Remove provisional CO sts when you come to them as described on page 8.)

To work border on long edges, PU 323 sts on each side edge and inc 1 st per edge for total of 324 sts. (See "Picking Up Stitches along a Side Edge" on page 9.)

You will have 15 border-patt reps on each end and 53 border-patt reps on side edges.

When you have reached end of border, knit 1 row so that needle points inward. PU 9 sts along edge of first corner so that needle points inward. Use Russian grafting (page 7) to join beginning and end of edging.

## FINISHING

Weave in ends. Block (page 10).

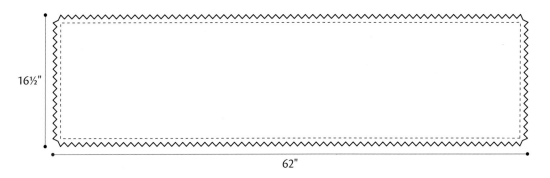

## Chart A

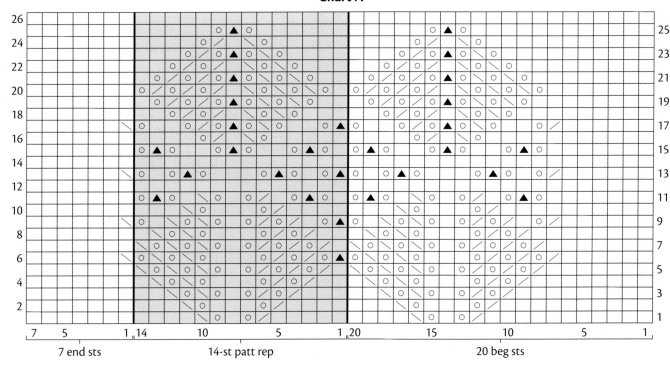

7 end sts        14-st patt rep        20 beg sts

## Chart B

## Key

| | K |
|---|---|
| − | P |
| ○ | YO |
| ╲ | ssk |
| ╱ | K2tog |
| ▲ | sl 1, K2tog, psso |

# TRIANGLES

Triangles are what many people first think of when they hear the word "shawls." Although the shape limits the design options, a knitted triangle makes a garment that drapes nicely and is comfortable to wear.

# margaret's lilacs in bloom
# TRIANGLE

This lightweight spring shawl evokes blooming lilacs. Margaret interpreted this theme with scattered flower motifs. This shawl is designed for beginning lace knitters; it's the perfect project for those who have never knit lace before. Although the pattern is long, it is very detailed, and if you follow it carefully step by step you should have no problem.

**Skill level:** ■■□□

**Dimensions:** 47" across top x 29" deep

**Gauge:** 7 sts and 10 rows = 1"

## MATERIALS

4 balls of 2-Ply Lace Yarn from Jamieson and Smith Shetland Wool Brokers (100% wool; 25 g; 185 yds) in color L136 (2)

Size 3 (3.25 mm) needles

Stitch markers

## SEED STITCH

*Worked over an odd number of sts:*

**All rows:** K1, *P1, K1, rep from * to end.

*Worked over an even number of sts:*

**Row 1:** *P1, K1, rep from * to end.

**Row 2:** *K1, P1, rep from * to end.

## SHAWL PATTERN

This shawl is worked with a 5-st-wide seed-st border all around. Once you've worked the first 5 rows of plain seed st, you'll begin to add YO increases to widen triangle and make room for lace motifs and garter st. You may find it helpful to use st markers to separate the first and last 5 sts of each row so that it's easy to remember to always work these sts in seed st.

CO 10 sts.

Beg working chart A (page 43). Rows 1–5 of border section are worked in seed st. Row 5 of seed-st border is WS row. You are now ready to start main patt, starting with row 1 (RS).

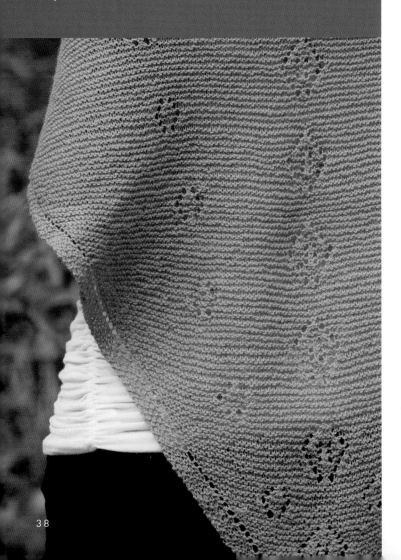

**Next row (RS):** Cont in patt, working seed-st edging, working YO inc inside each edging on odd-numbered rows, and working garter st (knit all sts) in bet for 18 rows—27 sts.

**Next RS row:** Work 5 seed-st edge sts, pm, YO, K2, pm, work row 1 of chart B (page 43), pm, YO, K2, pm, work 5 left-edge seed sts.

**Next WS row:** Work 5 seed-st edge sts, sl marker, K3, sl marker, knit row 2 of chart B, sl marker, K3, sl marker, work 5 seed sts.

Cont as est, working edge sts, knitting all sts bet markers, and completing all 18 rows of chart B.

Work 2 plain rows as foll: work 5 seed-st edge sts, YO (on RS row), knit to last 5 sts, YO (on RS row), work 5 seed-st edge sts—47 sts.

**Next RS row:** Work seed-st and YO edge patt, K7, work row 1 of chart C, K17, work row 1 of chart C, K7; work seed-st and YO edge patt.

Cont in patt, working all 10 rows of chart C.

Work 2 plain rows as foll: work 5 seed-st edge sts, YO (on RS row), knit to last 5 sts, YO (on RS row), work 5 seed-st edge sts—59 sts.

**Next RS row:** Work edge patt, K23, work row 1 of chart B, K23, work edge patt.

Cont in patt, working all 18 rows of chart B.

Work 2 plain rows as before.

**Next RS row:** Work edge patt, K14, work row 1 of chart C, K35, work row 1 of chart C, K14, work edge patt.

Cont as est until you've worked all rows of chart C.

Work 2 plain rows.

**Next RS row:** Work edge patt, K39, work row 1 of chart B, K39, work edge patt.

Cont as est, working all rows of chart B.

Work 2 plain rows.

**Next RS row:** Work edge patt, K23, work row 1 of chart C, K49, work row 1 of chart C, K23, work edge patt.

Cont as est until you've worked all rows of chart C.

Work 2 plain rows.

**Next RS row:** Work edge patt, K55, work row 1 of chart B, K55, work edge patt.

Cont as est until you've worked all rows of chart B.

Work 2 plain rows.

**Next RS row:** Work edge patt, K36, work row 1 of chart C, K55, work row 1 of chart C, K36, work edge patt.

Cont as est until you've worked all rows of chart C.

Work 2 plain rows.

**Next RS row:** Work edge patt, K71, work row 1 of chart B, K71 sts, work edge patt.

Cont as est until you've worked all rows of chart B.

Work 2 plain rows.

**Next RS row:** Work edge patt, K48, work row 1 of chart C, K69, work row 1 of chart C, K48, work edge patt.

Cont as est until you've worked all rows of chart C.

Work 2 plain rows.

**Next RS row:** Work edge patt, K87, work row 1 of chart B, K87, work edge patt.

Cont as est until you've worked all rows of chart B.

Work 2 plain rows.

**Next RS row:** Work edge patt, K61, work row 1 of chart C, K69, work row 1 of chart C, K61, work edge patt.

Cont as est until you've worked all rows of chart C.

Work 2 plain rows.

**Next RS row:** Work edge patt, K111, work row 1 of chart B, K111, work edge patt.

Cont as est until you've worked all rows of chart B.

Work 2 plain rows.

**Next RS row:** Work edge patt, K73, work row 1 of chart C, K77, work row 1 of chart C, K73, work edge patt.

Cont as est until you've worked all rows of chart C.

Work 2 plain rows.

**Next RS row:** Work edge patt, K119, work row 1 of chart B, K119, work edge patt.

Cont as est until you've worked all rows of chart B. Work 2 plain rows.

**Next RS row:** Work edge patt, K87, work row 1 of chart C, K81, work row 1 of chart C, K87, work edge patt.

Cont as est until you've worked all rows of chart C. Work 2 plain rows.

**Next RS row:** Work edge patt, K135, work row 1 of chart B, K135, work edge patt.

Cont as est until you've worked all rows of chart B. Work 2 plain rows.

**Next RS row:** Work edge patt, K103, work row 1 of chart C, K81, work row 1 of chart C, K103, work edge patt.

Cont as est until you've worked all rows of chart C. Work 2 plain rows.

**Next RS row:** Work edge patt, K151, work row 1 of chart B, K151, work edge patt.

Cont as est until you've worked all rows of chart B. Work 2 plain rows.

**Next RS row:** Work edge patt, (K2tog, YO) across, work edge patt.

**Next row:** Work even in seed-st patt (no more increases) for 5 rows.

BO loosely.

## FINISHING
Weave in ends. Block (page 10).

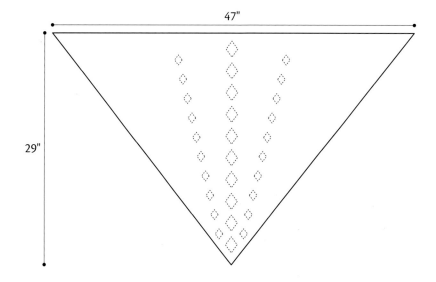

## Chart C

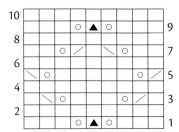

## Chart B

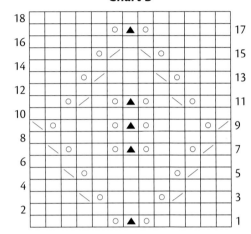

### Key

| | |
|---|---|
| ☐ | K (all rows) |
| • | K on RS, P on WS |
| — | P on RS, K on WS |
| ○ | YO |
| ╱ | K2tog |
| ╲ | ssk |
| ▲ | sl 1, K2tog, psso |
| ▨ | Seed-st edging |

## Chart A

6-st/2-row rep for edging     6-st/2-row rep for edging

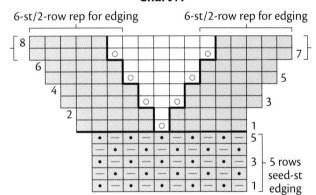

5 rows seed-st edging

# carol's
# SHAWL COLLAR
# triangle

This lovely but simple triangle is designed for beginning lace knitters, although certainly everyone can appreciate it. It increases from the center so you can easily make it larger by working additional repeat sections.

**Skill level:** ■■□□

**Dimensions:** 60" x 47"

**Gauge:** 7 sts and 8 rows = 1"

## MATERIALS

2 balls of Zephyr from JaggerSpun (50% merino wool, 50% tussah silk; 2 oz; 630 yds) in color Plum **2**

Size 2 (2.75 mm) needles

Stitch markers

## PATTERN

CO 2 sts. Work beg block of chart (12 rows) on page 47.

Work row 1 of vertical patt rep, placing st marker on either side of center YO. Cont working 12-row vertical rep, keeping st markers in place to keep first and last 7 sts separated from widening group of center sts.

After you've completed 12 rows of chart you should have 25 sts.

Beg row 1 of vertical rep again, but now work 1 beg st, 2 horizontal reps of 6-st edging, work center portion, work 2 more 6-st horizontal reps, and then work end st. You may find it helpful to separate each horizontal rep with a st marker.

Each time you beg new vertical rep, you will be working 1 more set of 6-st horizontal reps on each side of center YO.

Cont working 12-row vertical reps until you have 30 horizontal-rep sections from chart A on each side of center sts, ending shawl on row 12 of vertical rep block.

BO loosely.

## FINISHING

Weave in ends and block (page 10).

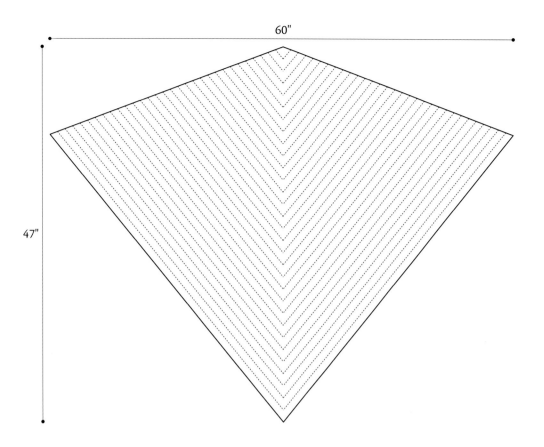

60"

47"

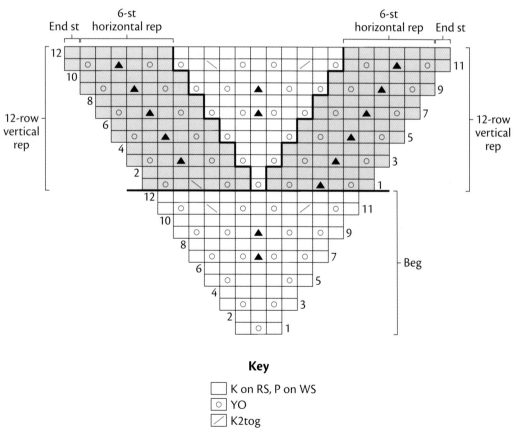

End st    6-st horizontal rep        6-st horizontal rep    End st

12-row vertical rep

12-row vertical rep

Beg

**Key**

☐ K on RS, P on WS

⊙ YO

╱ K2tog

╲ ssk

▲ sl 1, K2tog, psso

# margaret's spring breeze HEAD SCARF

Early flowers blowing in a light breeze, glittering from a spring rain—this is what I see in Margaret's design. Although the knitting of this beautiful piece is easy, the layout is complex, making this project a worthwhile challenge.

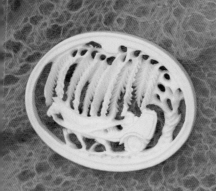

**Skill level:** ■■□□

**Dimensions:** 44" x 22½"

**Gauge:** 6 sts and 8 rows = 1"

## MATERIALS

2 balls of Douceur et Soie from Knit One, Crochet Too (65% baby mohair, 35% silk; 25 g; 225 yds) in color 8561 Soft Teal **1**

Size 3 (3.25 mm) needles

Stitch markers

Row/stitch counter

## PATTERN

CO 19 sts.

**Rows 1–16:** Work rows 1–16 of chart A (page 51).

**Rows 17–50:** Rep, working rows 3–16 of chart A and working edge reps on each side as you go until you've worked 50 rows—67 sts. (Note that for each rep of chart A, you will be adding another vertical column of YO and double decreases in your pattern.)

**Row 51:** Beg working chart B patt (page 51) as foll: work 29 sts across row as est, pm, work row 1 of chart B, pm, work 29 sts to end of row as est. (Chart B sts are inset into center of chart A sts.)

**Row 52:** Knit all sts.

**Rows 53–80:** Work chart B, maintaining edge sts in chart A patt.

**Rows 81–116:** Beg working chart C (page 52) on center 17 sts, meanwhile working sides of scarf as est in patts from charts A and B.

**Rows 117–158:** Keeping edges in patts from charts A and B, rep rows 103–116 of chart C 3 times, knitting all sts bet initial lace motif and center sts.

**Rows 159–164:** Work 6-row border using chart D (page 52), or as foll: on RS rows, K3, *YO, sl 1, K2tog, psso, YO, K3, rep from * to end. On WS rows, knit all sts.

BO loosely.

## FINISHING

Weave in ends. Do not block. Dry clean only.

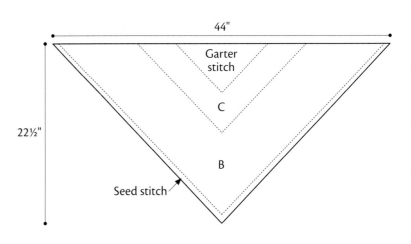

**Chart B**

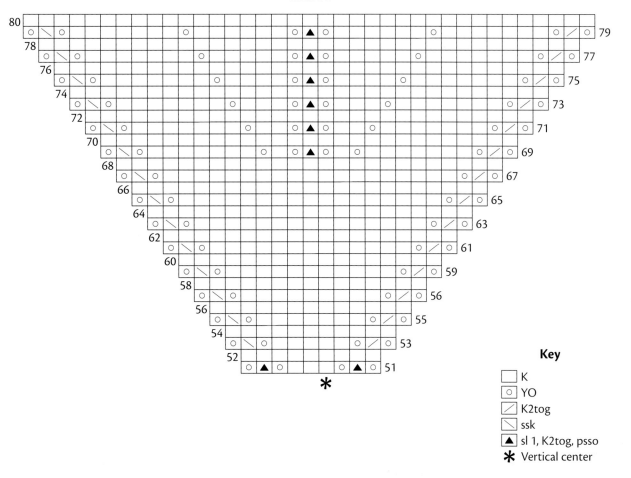

**Key**

- ☐ K
- ⊙ YO
- ╱ K2tog
- ╲ ssk
- ▲ sl 1, K2tog, psso
- ✳ Vertical center

**Chart A**

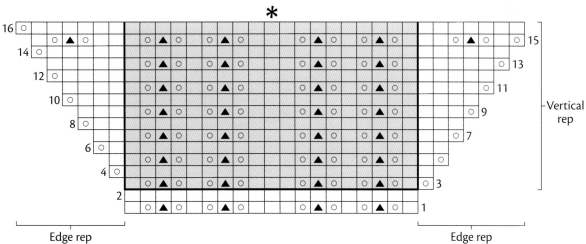

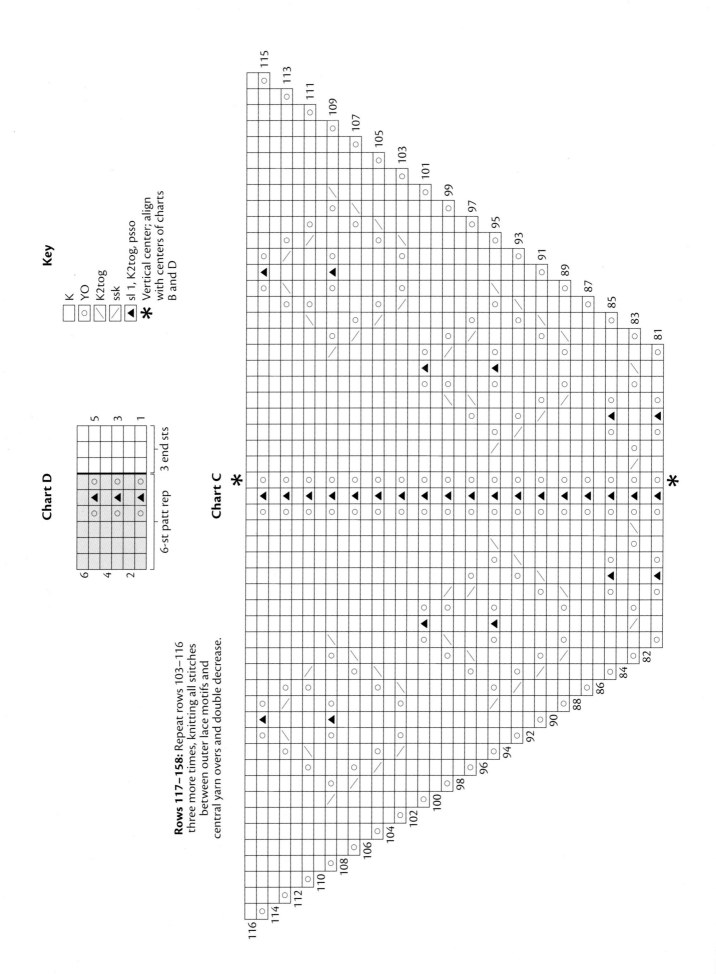

**Key**

| | |
|---|---|
| ☐ | K |
| ○ | YO |
| ╱ | K2tog |
| ╲ | ssk |
| ◄ | sl 1, K2tog, psso |
| * | Vertical center; align with centers of charts B and D |

**Chart D**

5
3
1

3 end sts

6-st patt rep

6
4
2

**Chart C**

**Rows 117–158:** Repeat rows 103–116 three more times, knitting all stitches between outer lace motifs and central yarn overs and double decrease.

# STOLES

Stoles can range from an airy little drape to a large, warm wrap. The secret to designing a stole that is comfortable to wear is to make it wide enough and long enough to wrap easily around the shoulders so that it'll stay put.

# carol's high country WRAP

Mountains upon mountains, high-country desert in winter: wrap yourself in the beautiful color of the land. Luxuriate in pure alpaca. This large, warm wrap will quickly become one of your favorite garments.

**Skill level:** ■■■□

**Dimensions:** 29" x 79½"

**Gauge:** 6¼ sts and 9¾ rows = 1"

## MATERIALS

4 balls of Alpaca Lace from Misti International (100% alpaca; 50 g; 437 m) in color Natural Tan **2**

Size 1 (2.25 mm) needles

Stitch markers

Waste yarn

## PATTERN

Using waste yarn, CO 150 sts for provisional CO (page 8).

Knit 6 rows.

Work first patt row of chart A (page 57) as foll: work 27 beg sts; pm; work 4 full patt reps (sts 1–24), pm bet patt reps; work 27 end sts.

Cont in patt, working 36 vertical patt reps. Work row 1 again.

On next WS row, knit across, purling second loops of double YOs.

Knit 6 rows. *Do not bind off.*

## BORDER

Referring to "Knitting On a Border" (page 9), CO 8 sts on end of needle with shawl stitches and begin working border patt foll chart B (page 56).

On top and bottom edges you will have 152 live sts and will work 26 border patt reps on these edges. (Take out provisional CO when you come to it.)

Work corners over 3 sts at beg and end of each edge, referring to "Working a Border Corner" (page 9).

To work border on long sides of wrap, PU 367 sts on each side edge. Dec 1 st bet corners on each long edge. You will have 62 border-patt reps on the side edges.

When you have reached end of border, knit 1 row so that needle points inward. PU 8 sts along edge of first corner so that needle points inward. Use Russian grafting (page 7) to join beginning and end of edging.

## FINISHING

Weave in all ends and block (page 10).

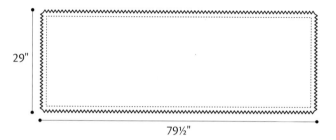

29"

79½"

### Chart B

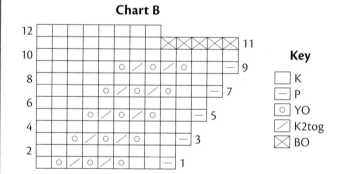

**Key**

- ☐ K
- − P
- ○ YO
- ╱ K2tog
- ☒ BO

**Chart A**

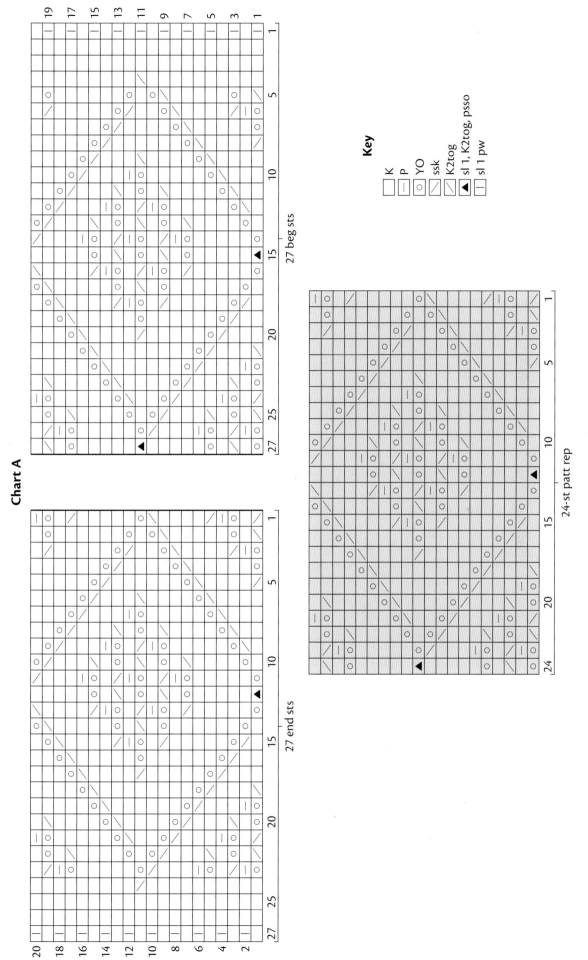

**Key**

| | K |
| :- | :- |
| $\mid$ | P |
| o | YO |
| / | ssk |
| \ | K2tog |
| ◄ | sl 1, K2tog, psso |
| $\mid$ | sl 1 pw |

27 beg sts

27 end sts

24-st patt rep

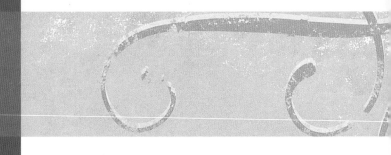

# carol's alice maud STOLE

This historical stitch pattern, named for Queen Victoria's second daughter, Alice Maud Mary (1843–1878), was first published in an early knitting manual from the 1840s. To complement the stole, I chose a traditional Shetland pattern called Queen's Edge for the border.

**Skill level:** ◀■■▢

**Dimensions:** 25" x 69"

**Gauge:** 5½ sts and 9 rows = 1"

## MATERIALS

2 balls of Zephyr from JaggerSpun (50% merino wool, 50% tussah silk; 2 oz; 630 yds) in color Aegean Blue 🎧 **2**

Size 2 (2.75 mm) needles

Stitch markers

Waste yarn

## PATTERN

Using waste yarn, CO 115 sts for provisional CO (page 8).

Knit 4 rows.

On next row set up patt referring to chart A (page 61) as foll: work 21 beg sts, pm, work 2 full reps of 36-st patt (pm bet), work 23 end sts.

Work as est until you've completed 28 vertical reps.

Knit 4 rows. *Don't bind off.*

## BORDER

Referring to "Knitting On a Border" (page 9), CO 6 sts onto needle with live sts and begin working border patt foll chart B (page 60).

On top and bottom edges you will have 115 live sts. Inc 5 sts bet corners so that you will have 12 reps of chart B. Work corners over 5 sts at beg and end of each edge.

On side edges, PU 284 sts on odd-numbered patt rows by picking up edge loop and twisting it to close up gap (see "Picking Up Stitches along a Side Edge" on page 9). These picked-up sts will be knit tog with last st of odd-numbered border rows to join border to stole. You will need to inc 6 sts bet corners along side edges so that you can work 26 patt reps along each side.

When you have reached end of border, knit 1 more row so that needle points inward. PU 6 sts along edge of first corner so that needle points inward. Use Russian grafting (page 7) to finish join.

## FINISHING

Weave in ends and block (page 10).

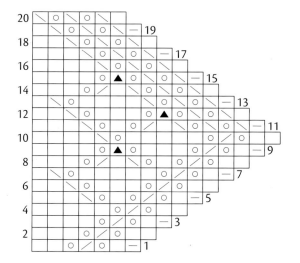

25"

69"

**Chart B**

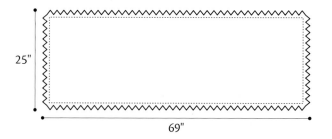

### Key

| | |
|---|---|
| ☐ | K |
| ⊟ | P |
| ⊡ | YO |
| ◻ | ssk |
| ◹ | K2tog |
| ▲ | sl 1, K2tog, psso |

**Chart A**

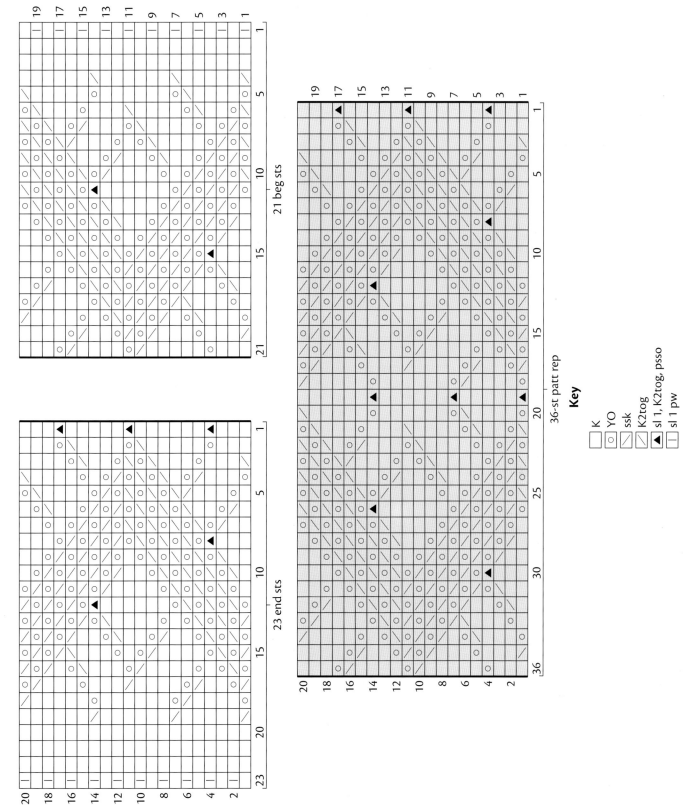

21 beg sts

23 end sts

36-st patt rep

**Key**

| | |
|---|---|
| ☐ | K |
| ○ | YO |
| ╱ | ssk |
| ╲ | K2tog |
| ◀ | sl 1, K2tog, psso |
| — | sl 1 pw |

# carol's alpine meadow STOLE

I love this color. Its hint of translucent lavender reminds me of morning light. So I designed a dewy alpine meadow scene. Ridges upon ridges of tall pines are surrounded by a carpet of alpine flowers.

**Skill level:** ■■■■

**Dimensions:** 27" x 76½"

**Gauge:** 5½ sts and 10 rows = 1"

## MATERIALS

3 balls of Zephyr from JaggerSpun (50% merino wool, 50% tussah silk; 2 oz; 630 yds) in color Pewter **2**

2 pairs of size 2 (2.75 mm) needles

50 stitch markers

Waste yarn

## SECTION 1

*Using waste yarn, CO 123 sts for provisional CO (page 8). Knit 8 rows.

Using chart A (page 65), set up first row of patt as foll: work 14 beg sts, pm, work four 24-st reps (pm bet patt reps), work 13 end sts.

Keeping in patt, work 3 vertical reps of 68-row patt.

Work rows 1 and 2 once more. Knit 2 rows.*

Using chart B (page 64), work as foll: work 12 edge sts, pm, work 8 reps of 12-st patt (pm bet patt reps), work 15 edge sts. Cont in patt until you have worked 25 vertical reps.

Knit 1 row. Leave sts on needle.

## SECTION 2

Work as for section 1 from * to *. Do not work chart B section. Leave sts on needle.

## JOINING

Align scarf sections with needles pointing toward one another and with wrong sides facing you. Join using Russian grafting (page 7).

## BORDER

Referring to "Knitting On a Border" (page 9), CO 8 sts and begin working border patt foll chart C below. Your piece will have a provisional CO at both top and bottom edges, where you will have 123 live sts. On top and bottom edges, dec 3 sts bet corners so that you can work 21 reps of chart C patt, below. Work corners over 3 sts at beg and end of each edge.

To work the border on long sides of stole, PU 364 sts stitches (see "Picking Up Stitches along a Side Edge" on page 9). You will need to dec 4 sts bet corners on side edges so that you can work 61 reps of chart C on side edges (see "Decreasing and Increasing along an Edge" on page 10).

When you have reached end of border, knit 1 more row so that needle points inward. PU 8 sts along edge of first corner so that needle points inward. Use Russian grafting (page 7) to finish join.

## FINISHING

Weave in ends and block (page 10).

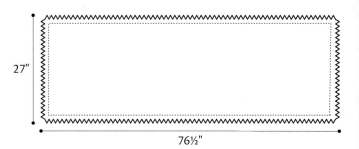

**Chart B**

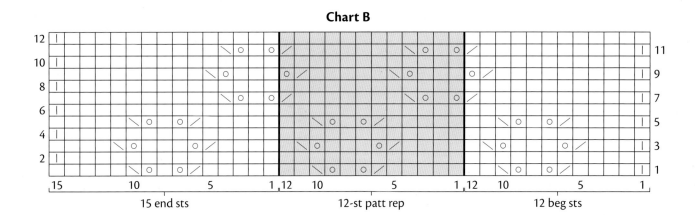

15 end sts          12-st patt rep          12 beg sts

**Chart C**

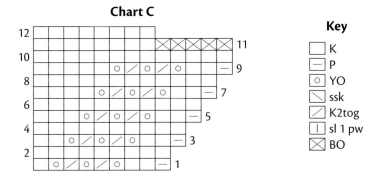

**Key**

☐ K
— P
○ YO
╲ ssk
╱ K2tog
| sl 1 pw
☒ BO

## Chart A

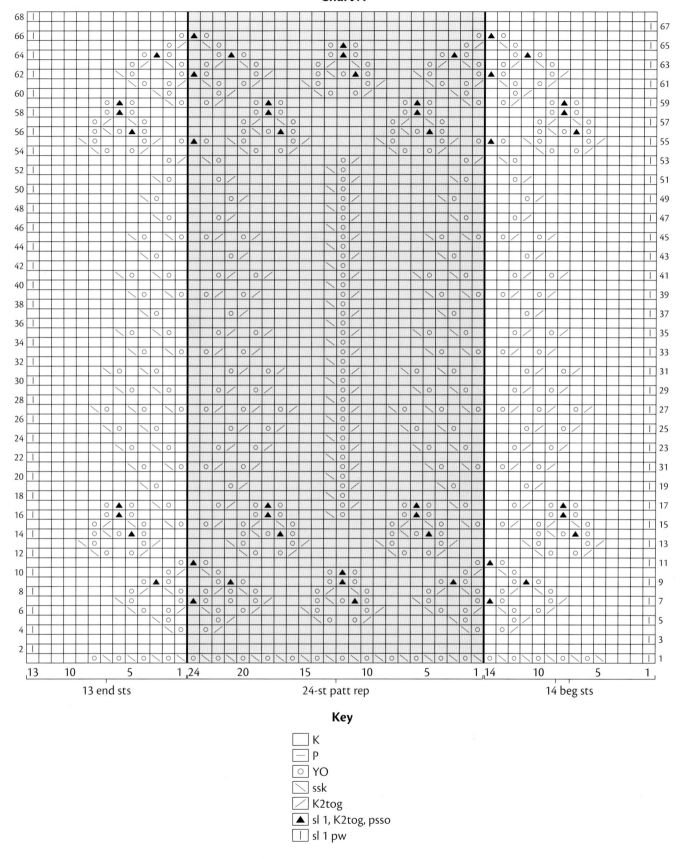

**Key**

- □ K
- ⊟ P
- ⊡ YO
- ◺ ssk
- ◹ K2tog
- ▲ sl 1, K2tog, psso
- Ⅰ sl 1 pw

# margaret's CAPE

Margaret created this stunningly beautiful cape by knitting individual pieces and then sewing them together. The border is sewn on after the pieces are joined. Although it looks complicated, it's actually quite simple to make, so don't be intimidated!

**Skill level:** ■■□□

**Back length:** 32" total; 25" with collar folded back

**Circumference:** 55" at bottom

**Gauge:** 5 sts and 10 rows = 1"

## MATERIALS

9 balls of 2-Ply Jumper Yarn from Jamieson and Smith Shetland Wool Brokers (100% wool; 25 g; 129 yds) in color Natural White [3]

Size 3 (3.25 mm) needles

Yarn needle

Stitch markers

## BODY PIECES (MAKE 5)

CO 84 sts.

Using chart A (page 68), set up first row as foll: work 12 beg sts; pm; work 5 reps of 12-st patt rep, pm bet each rep; work 12 end sts.

Work all rows of chart A. After 14 patterned rows, you'll have 72 sts. After 8 knit rows, you'll have 64 sts.

Foll chart B (page 68), set up first row as foll: work 8 beg sts, pm, work 4 horizontal reps of 12-st patt (pm bet), work 8 end sts.

Cont in patt, work all 16 rows of chart B.

To finish piece, knit all rows, dec 1 st each edge inside sl-st edge on 5th row and then on every 4th row until 10 sts remain. BO loosely.

## BODY ASSEMBLY

Lay out pieces with edges aligned and right sides facing. With yarn and yarn needle, interlace first from one edge and then from other through edge sl sts. When blocked, seaming will form herringbone. You will have 5 sections and 4 seams.

## BORDER

This border is knit separately and then sewn to cape.

CO 26 sts. Work 77 reps of chart C, below. BO loosely.

## FINISHING

Starting at lower-right edge, join border around body of cape using mattress or hem st, easing in fullness. Sew two ends of border together. Weave in ends. Block with pins instead of wires.

### Chart C

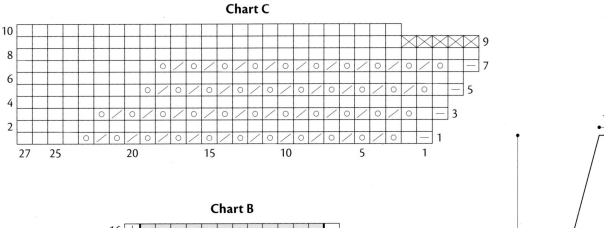

### Chart B

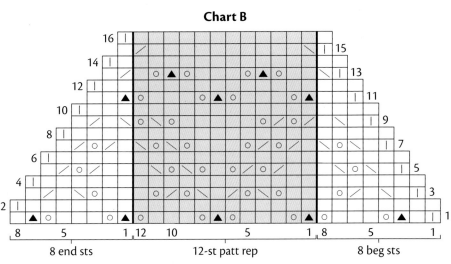

8 end sts · 12-st patt rep · 8 beg sts

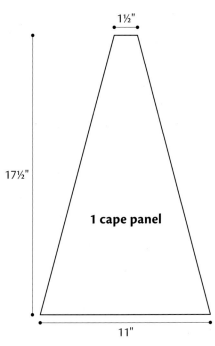

1½"

17½"

1 cape panel

11"

### Chart A

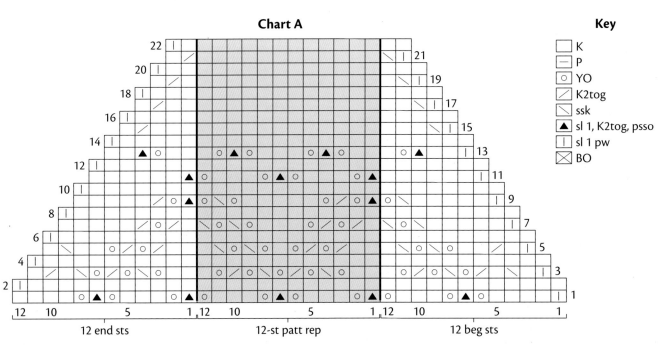

12 end sts · 12-st patt rep · 12 beg sts

### Key

| | |
|---|---|
| □ | K |
| − | P |
| ⊙ | YO |
| ╱ | K2tog |
| ╲ | ssk |
| ▲ | sl 1, K2tog, psso |
| I | sl 1 pw |
| ⊠ | BO |

# SQUARES

Squares are the ultimate in lace knitting. They can run from simple to complex in design, but in all cases they are luxurious to wear when folded into a triangle or when used as a blanket.

# carol's rosebuds
# BABY BLANKET or SHAWL

This luxurious lace square makes a treasured presentation baby blanket. But folded in half to form a triangle, it becomes a shawl that lets you always carry spring with you. It reminds me of an early spring morning after it's rained, when I wake to see the high desert carpeted with tiny pink flowers that are just the color of this shawl.

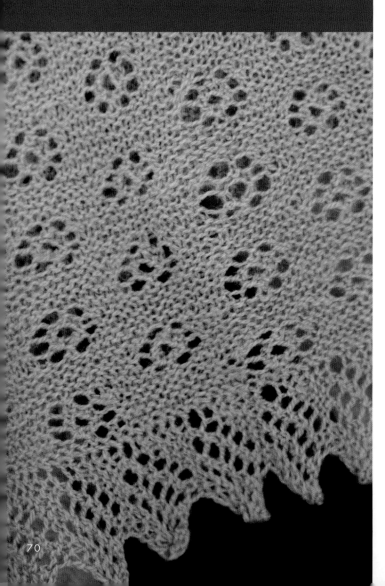

**Skill level:** ◼◼◻◻

**Dimensions:** 44" x 44"

**Gauge:** 5½ sts and 11 rows = 1"

## MATERIALS

3 balls of Zephyr from JaggerSpun (50% merino wool, 50% tussah silk; 2 oz; 630 yds) in color Cassis **2**

Size 2 (2.75 mm) needles

13 stitch markers

Waste yarn

## PATTERN

Using waste yarn, CO 209 sts for provisional CO (page 8). Foll chart A (page 73), work row 1 as foll: work first 11 beg sts; pm; work 12 reps of 16-st patt rep, pm bet; work 6 end sts.

Work in patt until you've completed 26 vertical patt reps. *Do not bind off.*

## BORDER

Referring to "Knitting On a Border" (page 9), CO 8 sts onto needle with live sts and begin working border patt foll chart B (page 73). You will have 209 live sts on top and bottom edges and will need to inc 1 st on each of these edges bet corners so that you are working border-patt rep across 210 sts. You'll have 36 patt reps on these edges. Work corners over 3 sts at beg and end of each edge. (Remove provisional CO sts as you come to them.)

To work border on side edges of baby blanket, PU 208 sts as you go on odd-numbered patt rows by picking up edge loop and twisting it to close up gap. (See "Picking Up Stitches along a Side Edge" on page 9). You will need to inc 2 sts bet corners so that you have a total of 210 sts. You will have 36 border-patt reps on each edge.

When you have reached end of border, knit 1 more row so that needle points inward. PU 8 sts along edge of first corner of border so that needle points inward. Use Russian grafting (page 7) to finish join.

## FINISHING

Weave in ends and block (page 10).

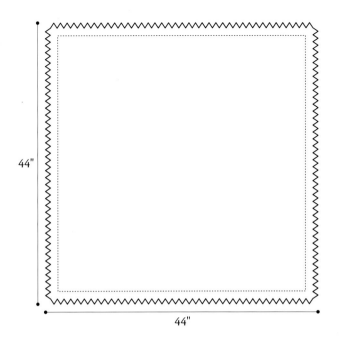

44"

44"

## Chart A

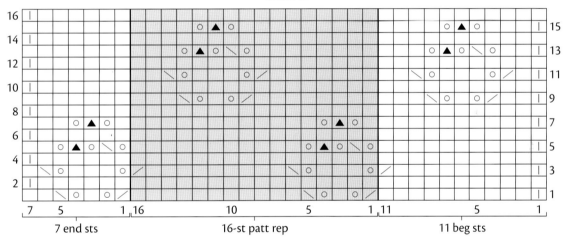

7 end sts    16-st patt rep    11 beg sts

## Chart B

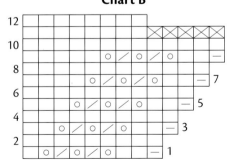

## Key

| | |
|---|---|
| ☐ | K |
| — | P |
| ○ | YO |
| ╱ | K2tog |
| ╲ | ssk |
| ▲ | sl 1, K2tog, psso |
| ⎮ | sl 1 pw |
| ⊠ | BO |

# carol's mardi gras
# SHAWL

These rich, festive colors put me in a Mardi Gras mood. This shawl requires the use of basic intarsia and careful counting, but the stitch patterns themselves are simple. Please don't be intimidated—once you get going, the instructions become clear. The shawl is knit in the Orenburg manner, which means it's knit from end to end, with the border knitted on afterwards.

**Skill level:** ■■■□

**Dimensions:** 56½" x 56½"

**Gauge:** 5½ sts and 10½ rows = 1"

## MATERIALS

Nature Spun Fingering from Brown Sheep Company (100% wool; 50 g; 310 yds) (3) in the following amounts and colors:

6 balls Husker Red

2 balls Plum Line

2 balls Peruvian Pink

Size 3 (3.25 mm) needles

Stitch markers

Waste yarn

## PATTERN

This shawl is worked back and forth, using the intarsia technique whenever more than one color is worked in a row. Refer to "Intarsia" (page 8) for more information before beginning the project. The border is knitted on after the center square is complete.

Using waste yarn, CO 272 sts for provisional CO (page 8). With red, knit 2 rows.

Using chart A (page 77), set up patt on next row as foll: work 16 beg sts; pm; work 15 reps of 16-st patt rep, pm bet each rep; work 16 end sts. Cont in patt, work 6 vertical reps of chart A.

On next RS row, work across 16 beg sts and 2 more horizontal patt reps in red. Tie on purple and use it to knit all sts across to beg of last 3 red reps (176 sts). Over these sts, inc 4 sts evenly spaced (180 purple sts). Tie on second ball of red and work 2 horizontal patt reps and 16 end sts of chart A. Cont working with red in chart A patt and AT SAME TIME knit 12 rows purple.

On next RS row, cont working chart A patt in red areas; with purple, work 16 horizontal reps of 11-st patt rep from chart B (page 78), pm bet; work 4 end sts. (The patt rep in corners of purple area are also first vertical reps of purple side borders as indicated on chart B.) After completing 1 vertical rep of chart B, knit 12 rows purple while AT SAME TIME cont to work vertical reps of chart B on first and last motifs in purple border band.

On next RS row, work in patt over red area; work in patt over 15 purple sts; tie on pink. With pink, knit across 150 purple sts, dec 5 sts evenly spaced (145 total pink sts). You should have 15 purple sts rem. Tie on second ball of purple and work across purple and red areas in patt.

On next WS row, cont in patt, knitting all pink sts.

On next RS row, set up pink patt from chart C (page 78) as foll: work 16 beg sts, pm, work 9 horizontal reps of chart C patt (pm bet), work 3 end sts. Cont in patt for each color, while working 12 vertical reps of chart C in pink. Work rows 1 and 2 of chart C again.

On next RS row, work red area in patt; work 15 sts of purple in patt; with purple, knit across all pink sts, inc 5 sts evenly spaced. Cut off second purple ball and cont across rem 15 purple sts with working purple yarn. Work red area in patt.

Maintaining patt, knit 12 rows purple, AT SAME TIME working first and last motif patt.

On next RS row, set up patt over purple from chart B as foll: work 16 horizontal reps of chart B, pm bet; work 4 end sts. Work 1 vertical rep of chart B patt across horizontal area. Knit 11 rows in purple, maintaining

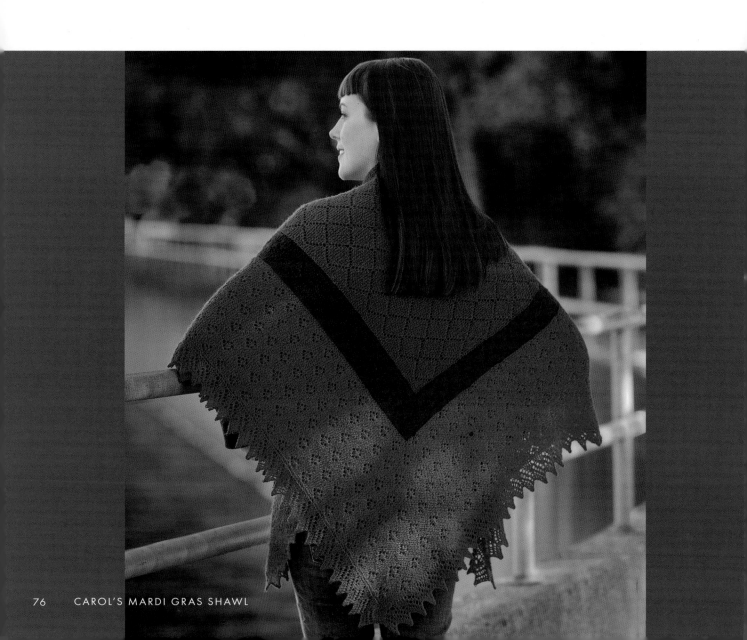

patt in red areas. On next row, dec 4 sts evenly spaced across purple area. Cut off purple. On next RS row, work across in red as for first horizontal border. Cut off second ball of red and work with 1 ball. Work 6 vertical reps of chart A. Knit 2 rows. *Do not bind off.*

## BORDERS

Referring to "Knitting On a Border" (page 9), CO 8 sts with red and beg working border patt foll chart D (page 78). On top and bottom edges you will have 272 sts. PU 274 sts on each side edge. Work corners over first and last 3 sts of each edge. On top and bottom edges dec 2 sts bet corners; on side edges dec 4 sts bet corners. You will have 46 reps of chart D on each edge. When you have reached end of border, knit 1 more row so needle points inward. PU 8 sts on edge of first corner so that needle points inward. Use Russian grafting (page 7) to finish join.

## FINISHING

Weave in ends and block (page 10).

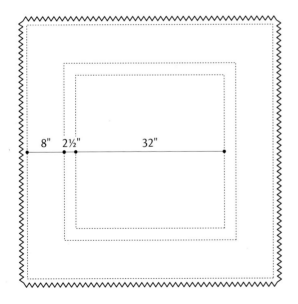

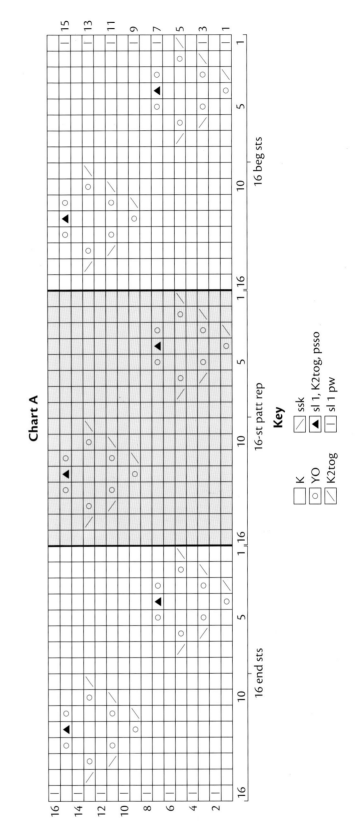

**Chart A**

16 beg sts

16-st patt rep

16 end sts

**Key**

| | | |
|---|---|---|
| ☐ K | ╱ ssk | |
| ◦ YO | ◄ sl 1, K2tog, psso | |
| ╲ K2tog | ─ sl 1 pw | |

## Chart B

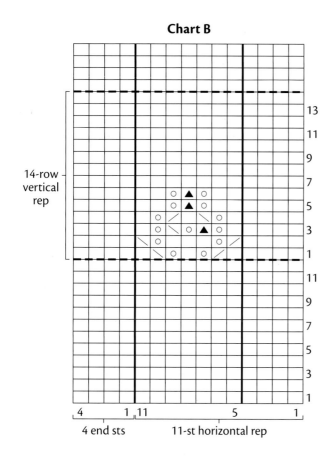

**14-row vertical rep**

4 | 1 | 11 | 5 | 1

4 end sts

11-st horizontal rep

## Key

- ☐ K
- ▭ P
- ○ YO
- ╱ K2tog
- ╲ ssk
- ▲ sl 1, K2tog, psso
- │ sl 1 pw
- ☒ BO

## Chart D

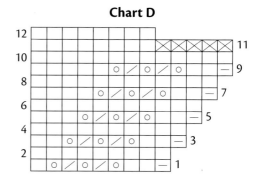

## Chart C

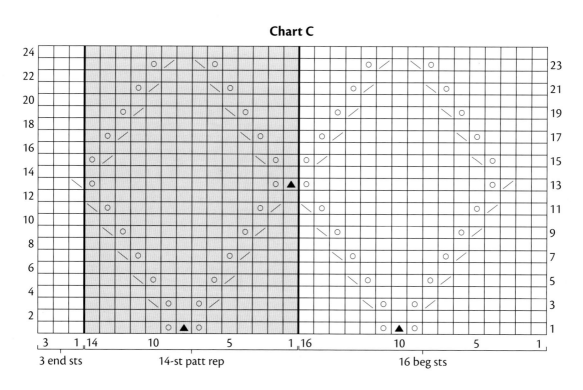

3 | 1 | 14 | 10 | 5 | 1 | 16 | 10 | 5 | 1

3 end sts

14-st patt rep

16 beg sts

# abbreviations

| | |
|---|---|
| beg | begin(ning) |
| bet | between |
| BO | bind off |
| CO | cast on |
| cont | continue(ing) |
| dec | decrease(ing)(s) |
| EOR | every other row |
| est | established |
| foll | follow(s) (ing) |
| g | gram(s) |
| inc | increase(ing) |
| K | knit |
| K2tog | knit 2 stitches together—1 stitch decreased |
| mm | millimeter(s) |
| oz | ounce(s) |
| P | purl |
| P2tog | purl 2 stitches together—1 stitch decreased |
| patt(s) | pattern(s) |
| pm | place marker |
| PU | pick up |
| pw | purlwise |
| rem | remain(ing) |
| rep | repeat |
| RS | right side |
| sl | slip |
| sl 1, K2tog, psso | slip 1 stitch purlwise, knit next 2 stitches together, then pass the slipped stitch back over the knit stitch and drop it off the needle—2 stitches decreased |
| ssk | slip, slip, knit: slip 1 stitch knitwise, slip second stitch knitwise, insert left needle into both slipped stitches and knit them together—1 stitch decreased |
| st(s) | stitch(es) |
| tog | together |
| WS | wrong side |
| yds | yard(s) |
| YO | yarn over |

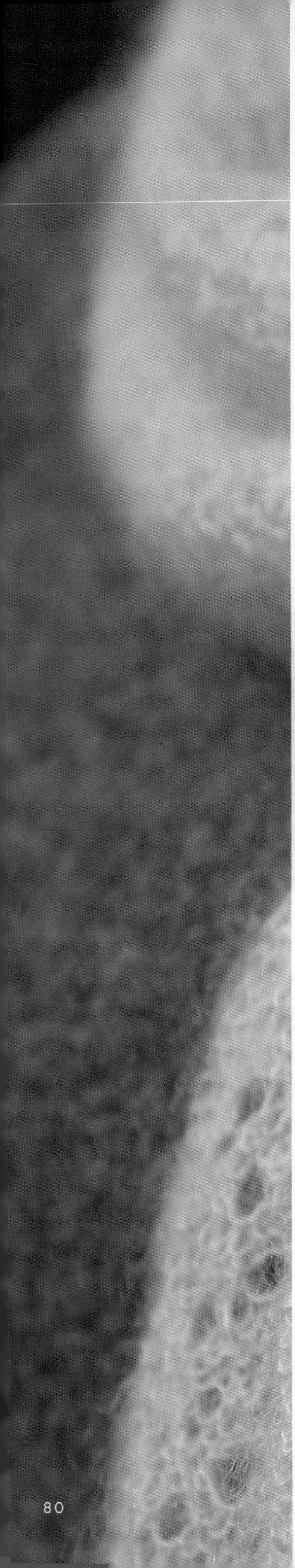

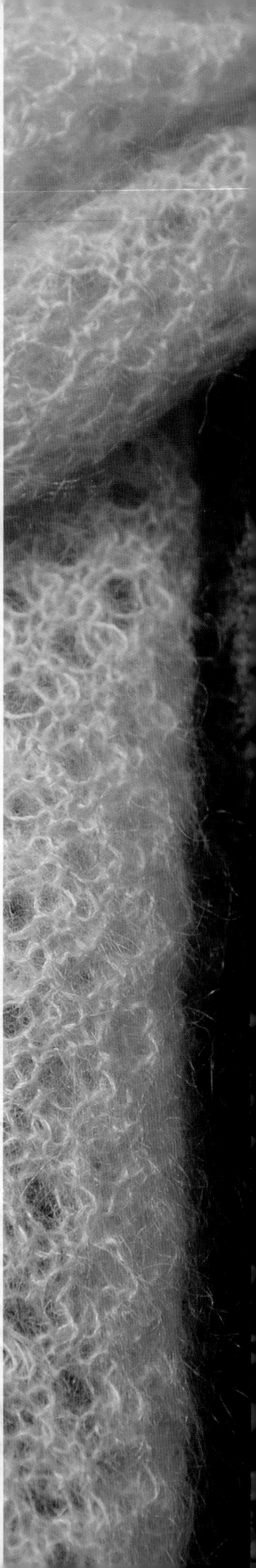

# resources

**BROWN SHEEP COMPANY**

1-800-826-9136

www.brownsheep.com


**JAGGERSPUN**

1-207-324-5622

www.jaggeryarn.com


**JAMIESON AND SMITH SHETLAND WOOL BROKERS**

011-441-595-693-579

www.shetland-wool-brokers.zetnet.co.uk


**KNIT ONE, CROCHET TOO**

1-800-357-7646

www.knitonecrochettoo.com


**MISTI INTERNATIONAL**

1-888-776-9276

www.mistialpaca.com